MARVIn the MOOSE

by David Strauss

Be Happy and Stay Positive!

Illustrated by Sonia Merkel

For my girls
Thanks for showing me that anything can be accomplished through love, passion, and imagination.

Copyright © David Strauss 2023
All rights reserved.

ISBN 979-8-218-18180-2

It was a beautiful morning in the northern woods of Maine, where many woodland creatures lived and played. One creature that enjoyed the splendor of Maine was Marvin the Moose.

Marvin was a gentle giant who enjoyed all the beauty around him. He lived by a flowing stream just on the outskirts of a beautiful field of wildflowers, and as such, he took in the splendor of his surroundings.

Most days Marvin was a happy fellow. He would start his day by going down to the stream for a refreshing gulp of water and then wander across the field of wildflowers, taking deep breaths of the sweet smells in the air.

After taking a leisurely stroll through the field of wildflowers, Marvin would continue his day by taking an afternoon nap under the shade of the mighty Maine pine trees.

Marvin would often stop to appreciate the beautiful surroundings that he called home, and this made Marvin extremely happy.

He stood at a distance, watching in fear as the lumberjack began to chop down the mighty Maine pines that towered over the field of wildflowers.

As Marvin watched the lumberjack destroy the pines, he started to reminisce about all the hot summer afternoons he had spent napping in the cool shade of those trees.

Unable to bear the sight of another pine falling, Marvin turned and retreated into the safety of the thick Maine woods, feeling heartbroken and helpless.

As Marvin made his way back to the stream, he was suddenly overtaken with a feeling of anger. "How dare that lumberjack cut down those trees that provided me with a cool place to take my afternoon naps"! For this was Marvin's home, the place that had always brought him comfort and happiness.

As the days went by, more and more trees were taken down, leaving nothing but barren land in their wake. Marvin couldn't help but feel a deep sense of gloom at the destruction of his once-beautiful home.

Despite his loss, Marvin was a happy fellow, and he worked to maintain his cheerful spirit.

Marvin carried on with his normal routines, maintaining a positive attitude and hoping that something beautiful would take the place of the trees that had once provided him with shade.

As the weeks went by, Marvin found himself unable to even think about going over to the barren land that had once brought him so much peace and happiness.

Marvin suddenly realized that he no longer heard the buzz of the lumberjack's chainsaw.

With the support of his woodland friends, Marvin mustered up the courage to explore the barren land.

The area that was once covered with pines was now a sea of wild Maine blueberries, their plump, juicy berries glistening in the sun. Marvin's eyes widened with wonder and joy as he took in the sight.

Marvin then realized that life is full of unexpected twists and turns, and that by staying positive and open-minded, we can find happiness and meaning in even the most challenging situations.

Marvin was grateful for the opportunity to discover something new and exciting. He felt that the blueberries were a symbol of hope and resilience, a reminder that even when things seem gloomy, there is always the potential for growth and renewal.

Although Marvin can no longer cool off under the shade of the mighty Maine pine, he now has a place to visit when craving a sweet treat.

Made in the USA
Middletown, DE
29 May 2024

54963250R00018